To

....

From

....

Date

....

A Note from Shanna Noel

Parenting is one of my greatest joys in life! Jonathan and I have two girls—and I cherish every single day I get to be a part of their lives. I love the conversations that come from sitting at our local coffee shop, hiking in the fall leaves, or late-night hang-outs at the foot of their bed. I often wish I could capture these treasured talks and keep them forever!

This journal was created to help spark conversations between mothers and daughters—conversations that are authentic, honest, and open. It's important to be vulnerable in a way that allows our kids to see how messy our faith can be at times, and it's equally important for them to see how we can withstand anything with God by our side.

I started a similar journal with my oldest daughter, Jaden, a few years back. We would sneak the journal underneath each other's door after we finished filling it out. I loved hearing her little feet run up and slip it under the door. She knew I was praying for her; she knew I was on her side; and she knew we were in this together; and that brought me comfort. I hope this journal does the same for you and your daughter.

xo
—Shanna
mom

I love having projects like this that help me to have time with my Mom and get to know her in a new way! –Addison, daughter

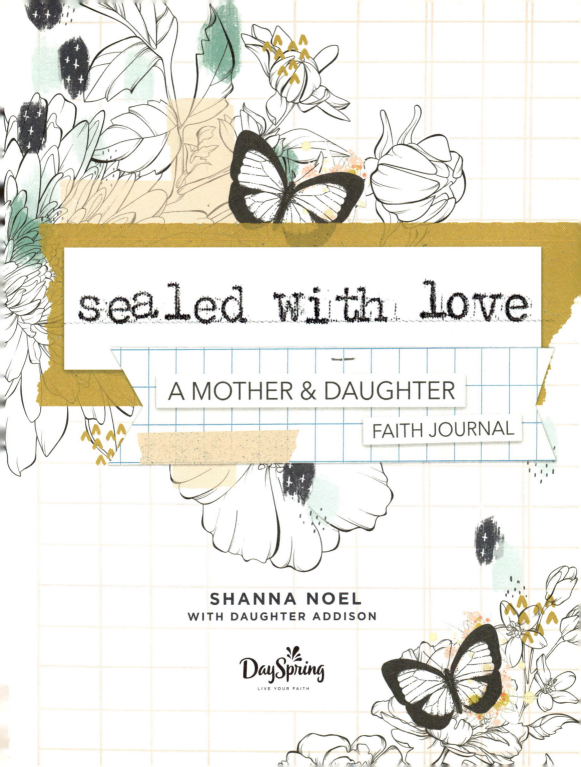

sealed with love

A MOTHER & DAUGHTER

FAITH JOURNAL

SHANNA NOEL
WITH DAUGHTER ADDISON

DaySpring
LIVE YOUR FAITH

1 Have you ever doubted God but kept it to yourself?

My prayer:

1 Have you ever doubted God but kept it to yourself?

date//

My prayer:

MOTHER

·daughter·

date//

2 What did you
imagine God
to be like when you were little,
and how is that different
from what you imagine now?

date//

2 What did you imagine God to be like when you were little, and how is that different from what you imagine now?

Prayer request:

·daughtER·

date//

3 When was the last time you opened your Bible, and what did you

discover?

Praise report!

date//

3 When was the last time you opened your Bible, and what **did you discover?**

Praise report!

♥MOTHER♥

·daughtER·

date//

4 Has it ever been awkward for you to pray, and if so, what do you do when that happens?

My prayer:

date//

4 Has it ever been awkward
for you **to pray,** and if so,
what do you do when that happens?

My prayer:

♥MOTHER♥

·daughtER·

date//

5 What was the last lesson
God taught you?

Prayer request:

date//

5 What was the last lesson God taught you?

Prayer request:

♥MOTHER♥

date//

6 Tell me about
the last time
God surprised you.

Praise report!

date//

6 Tell me
about the last time
God surprised you.

Praise report!

·daughtER·

date//

7 Which Scripture
in the Bible is inspiring you today?

My prayer:

date//

7 Which Scripture in the Bible is inspiring you today?

My prayer:

♥MOTHER♥

date//

8 What do you imagine your life
will look like
in 10 years?

Prayer request:

date//

8 What do you imagine
your life will look like
in 10 years?

Prayer request:

♥MOTHER♥

·daughtER·

date//

9 If you could ask God
one question,
what would it be?

Praise report!

date//

9 If you could
ask God one question,
what would it be?

Praise report!

♥MOTHER♥

·daughter·

date//

10 What are 5 things you do
that make you feel
most connected to God?

My prayer:

date//

10 What are 5 things you do that make you feel most connected to God?

My prayer:

·daughtER·

date//

11

Write some of the lyrics
to one of your favorite worship songs.

Prayer request:

date//

11 Write some of the lyrics
to one of your favorite
worship songs.

Prayer request:

♥MOTHER♥

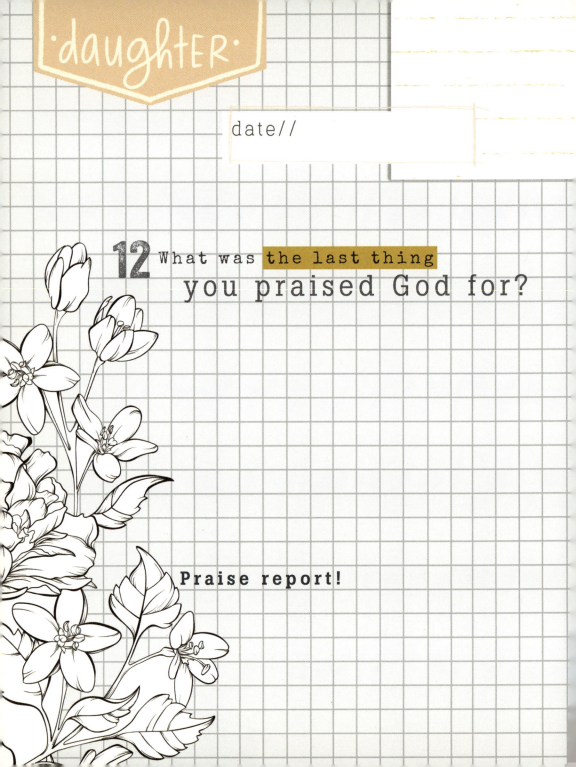

·daughtER·

date//

12 What was the last thing you praised God for?

Praise report!

12 What was the last thing
you praised God for?

Praise report!

MOTHER

date//

13 Random act
of kindness challenge!

Share one random act of kindness
you do in the next 24 hours.

My prayer:

date//

13 Random act of kindness challenge! Share one random act of kindness you do in the next 24 hours.

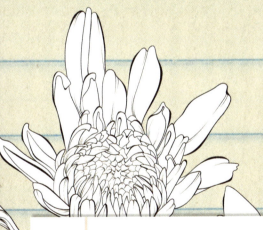

My prayer:

·daughtER·

date//

14 When was the last time you prayed for someone?

Prayer request:

date//

14 When was the last time you prayed for someone?

Prayer request:

·daughter·

date//

15 Tell me about a dream
God has recently placed
on **your heart.**

Praise report!

15 Tell me about a dream
God has recently placed
on your heart.

Praise report!

MOTHER

date//

16

Finish this sentence:
I know God has

a sense of humor
because...

My prayer:

date//

16

Finish this sentence:
I know God has
a **sense of humor** because...

My prayer:

♥MOTHER♥

date//

17 Free space!

Use the space below to ask questions
or share a new idea!

Prayer request:

date//

Prayer request:

MOTHER

date//

18 What are 3 goals
you want to work on
to make God a priority?

Praise report!

date//

18 What are 3 goals
you want to work on
to make God a priority?

Praise report!

♥MOTHER♥

·daughtER·

date//

19

What in `nature` **connects you most to God?**

(fill in the bubble)

o Trees

o Stars

o Animals

o Flowers

o Scenery

o Sunset

o Sunrise

o _____

My prayer:

19 What in nature connects you most to God?

(fill in the bubble)

o Trees

o Stars

o Animals

o Flowers

o Scenery

o Sunset

o Sunrise

o _____

My prayer:

♥ MOTHER ♥

·daughter·

date//

20

What is something you think
people your age
struggle with
in their faith?

Prayer request:

20 What is something you think people your age struggle with in their faith?

Prayer request:

·daughter·

date//

21

Has there ever been a time you've <mark>struggled</mark> to share your faith?

Praise report!

date//

21 Has there ever been a time
you've struggled to share your faith?

Praise report!

·daughter·

date//

22 Free space!
Use the space below to ask questions
or share a new idea!

My prayer:

date//

My prayer:

date//

23 What does this verse
teach us about God?

Children are a gift from the Lord.
Babies are a reward.
PSALM 127:3 ICB

Prayer request:

date//

23 What does this verse
teach us about God?

Children are a gift from
the Lord. Babies are a reward.
PSALM 127:3 ICB

Prayer request:

♥ MOTHER ♥

·daughter·

date//

24

What is one of your
favorite memories
about the two of us?

Praise report!

date//

24 What is one of your favorite memories about the two of us?

Praise report!

MOTHER

·daughter·

date//

25 When was the last time you talked about God in front of your friends?

My prayer:

25 When was the last time you **talked about God** in front of your friends?

My prayer:

MOTHER

·daughtER·

⁺⁺⁺

date//

26

When was the last time you
forgave someone and why?

Prayer request:

date//

26 When was the last time you forgave someone and why?

Prayer request:

MOTHER

·daughtER·

date//

27 Finish this sentence:
One of the things
I love most about you is...

Praise report!

date//

27

Finish this sentence:
One of the things I love most
about you is...

Praise report!

MOTHER

·daughter·

date//

28 What is a promise in the Bible
that helps you
when you need hope?

My prayer:

date//

28

What is a promise
in the Bible that helps you
when you need hope?

My prayer:

·daughter·

date//

29 Free space!

Use the space below to ask questions or share a new idea!

Prayer request:

date//

Prayer request:

♥MOTHER♥

date//

30 What is something you need
to surrender to Jesus?

Praise report!

date//

30 What is something you need to surrender to Jesus?

Praise report!

MOTHER

·daughtER·

date//

31 Tell me about a time you felt covered by God's peace.

My prayer:

date//

31 Tell me about a time you felt covered by God's peace.

My prayer:

date//

32 Free space!

Use the space below to ask questions
or share a new idea!

Prayer request:

date//

Prayer request:

date//

33 If you could
ask Jesus one question,
what would it be?

Praise report!

33 If you could ask Jesus one question, what would it be?

Praise report!

MOTHER

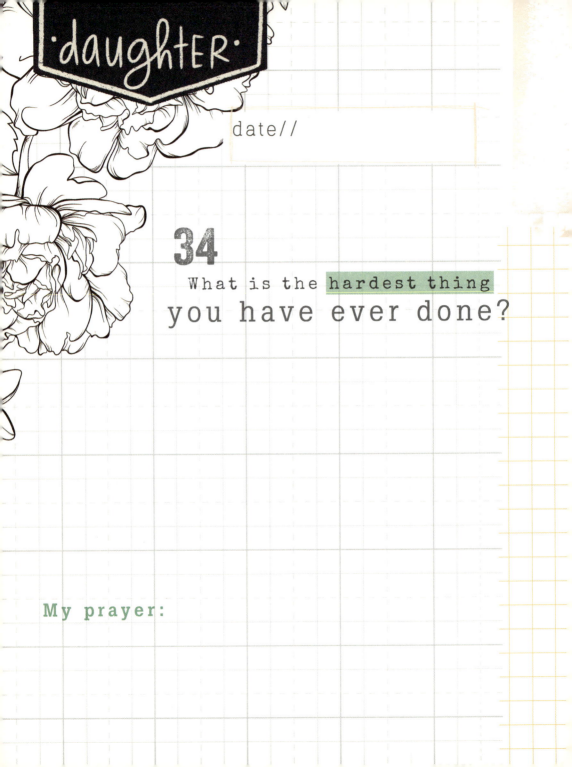

·daughtER·

date//

34

What is the hardest thing you have ever done?

My prayer:

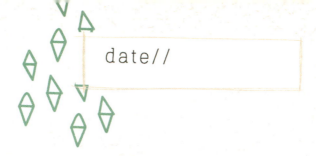

date//

34 What is the hardest thing you have ever done?

My prayer:

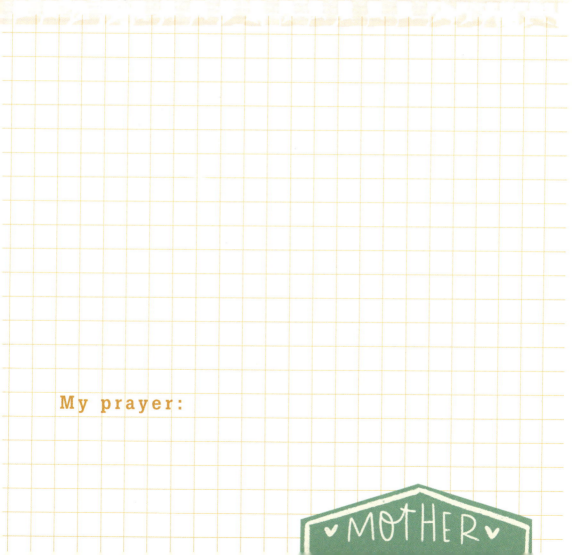

♥MOTHER♥

date//

35

Finish this sentence:

Something
I hope to do
one day is...

Prayer request:

date//

35 Finish this sentence:
Something I hope
to do one day is...

Prayer request:

·daughter·

date//

36 How would you define faith?

Praise report!

36 How would you define faith?

Praise report!

date//

37 What are **4 gifts** you think
God has given you?

My prayer:

37 What are 4 gifts you think God has given you?

My prayer:

♥MOTHER♥

·daughtER·

date//

38 How can you use
those gifts
to glorify God?

Prayer request:

date//

38 How can you use those gifts to glorify God?

Prayer request:

date//

39
Is there an area
in your life you need
to trust God more?

Praise report!

date//

39 Is there an area in your life you need to **trust God more?**

Praise report!

·daughtER·

date//

40 When do you feel
closest to God?

My prayer:

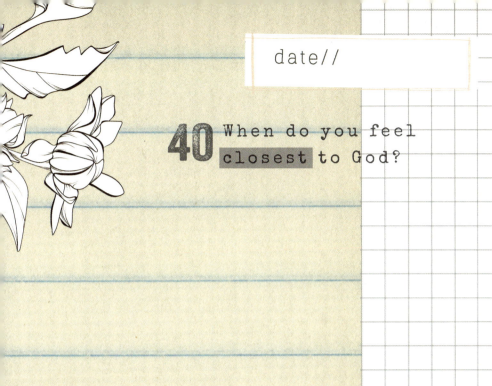

date//

40 When do you feel closest to God?

My prayer:

♥MOTHER♥

·daughtER·

date//

41

When do you feel farthest from God?

Prayer request:

date//

41 When do you feel **farthest** from God?

Prayer request:

♥MOTHER♥

date//

42 Can you remember the first time you felt Jesus in your heart?

Praise report!

42 Can you remember the first time you felt Jesus in your heart?

Praise report!

MOTHER

date//

43 Describe your perfect day.

My prayer:

date//

43 Describe your perfect day.

My prayer:

·daughtER·

date//

44 What **motivates** you?

Prayer request:

date//

44 What motivates you?

Prayer request:

MOTHER

date//

45 How do you pray differently now than when you were younger?

Praise report!

date//

45 How do you pray differently now than when you were younger?

♥MOTHER♥

date//

46

What are some of your favorite ways
to serve others?

My prayer:

date//

46 What are some of
your favorite ways
to serve others?

My prayer:

♥MOTHER♥

·daughtER·

date//

47 What does it mean to love God?

Prayer request:

date//

47 What does it mean to love God?

♥MOTHER♥

48 List some of your
favorite ways
to share your faith.

Praise report!

date//

48

List some of your **favorite ways** to share your faith.

Praise report!

♥MOTHER♥

·daughtER·

date//

49 Free space!
Use the space below
to ask questions
or share a new idea!

My prayer:

date//

My prayer:

·daughtER·

date//

50 Have you ever felt
distant from God?
What did you do to get closer?

Prayer request:

date//

50 Have you ever <mark>felt distant</mark> from God? What did you do to get closer?

Prayer request:

MOTHER

date//

51 Besides family,
which people in your life
have had the most impact
on your faith?

Praise report!

date//

51 Besides family, which people in your life have had the most impact on your faith?

Praise report!

date//

52

What do you do when you have
doubts about your faith?

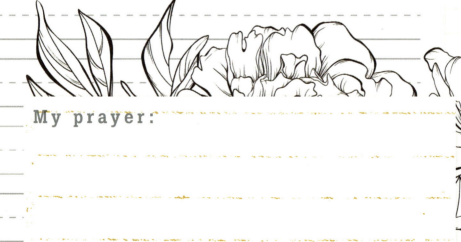

My prayer:

52 What do you do when you have **doubts** about your faith?

My prayer:

·daughtER·

date//

53Free space!

Use the space below to ask questions
or share a new idea!

Prayer request:

date//

Prayer request:

MOTHER

·daughtER·

date//

54

What are some
of your favorite ways
to connect with God?
(fill in the bubble)

o Reading My Bible

o Church

o Youth Group

o Prayer

Praise report!

o Journaling

o Worship

o Communion

o Fellowship

o Serving Others

o _____

date//

54 What are some of your favorite ways to **connect with God?**
(fill in the bubble)

o Reading My Bible

o Church

o Small Group

o Prayer

o Journaling

o Worship

o Communion

o Fellowship

o Serving Others

o _____

Praise report!

♥MOTHER♥

date//

55 How would you define grace?

My prayer:

55 How would you define grace?

My prayer:

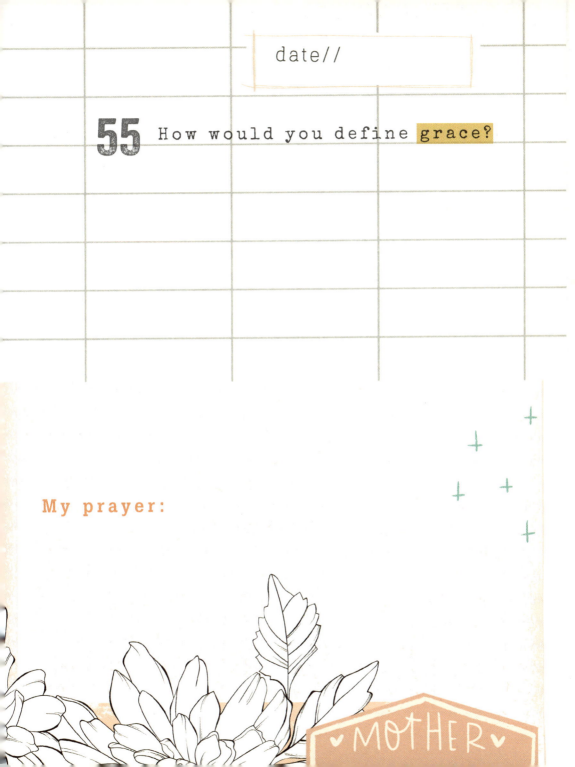

MOTHER

date//

56 If our family
was a movie,
what would it be called?

Prayer request:

date//

56

If our family was a movie, what would it be called?

Prayer request:

·daughtER·

date//

57 What do you think heaven is like?

✝✝ Praise report!

date//

57 What do you think heaven is like?

Praise report!

·daughter·

date//

58 What is your favorite
Bible story?

My prayer:

58 What is your favorite Bible story?

My prayer:

·daughtER·

date//

59 What do you think we could do **as a family** to make the world **a better place?**

Prayer request:

date//

59 What do you think we could do as a family to make the world a better place?

Prayer request:

·daughtER·

date//

60 What is the **hardest thing** about being your age?

Praise report!

date//

60 What is the hardest thing about being your age?

Praise report!

MOTHER

date//

61
What is the best thing
about being your age?

My prayer:

date//

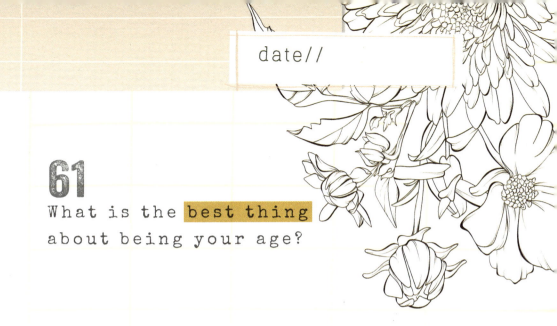

61

What is the **best thing** about being your age?

My prayer:

·daughtER·

date//

62 What was
the most surprising thing
you learned as we worked
through this journal?

Prayer request:

date//

62 What was the `most surprising` thing you learned as we worked through this journal?

Prayer request:

Sealed with Love: A Mother and Daughter Faith Journal
Copyright © 2020 by Shanna Noel
First Edition, May 2020

Published by:

21154 Highway 16 East
Siloam Springs, AR 72761
dayspring.com

Written and Designed by: Shanna Noel

Printed in Korea
Prime: J2030
ISBN: 978-1-64454-632-1